The study of the violin presents certain difficulties for beginners which are frequently the cause of a sudden abatement in the pupil's zeal and ambition, even before he has mastered the first rudiments.

The blame for this is commonly laid on the teacher, who is called incapable or negligent; losing sight of the fact that the pupil began his studies without the slightest notion, not merely of the difficulties to be encountered, but also of the regular and assiduous industry indispensable for surmounting them.

It is important, therefore, to smooth these first asperities by showing their utility and making them agreeable; to this end my Violin Method was published and the present Exercises have been written, which latter may be considered as forming a supplement to the former.

If practiced carefully and intelligently, they will serve as a solid foundation for the technique of any player ambitious to become an artist.

Franz Wohlfahrt

No. 1

Wohlfahrt
Op. 45, No. 1

Allegro Moderato

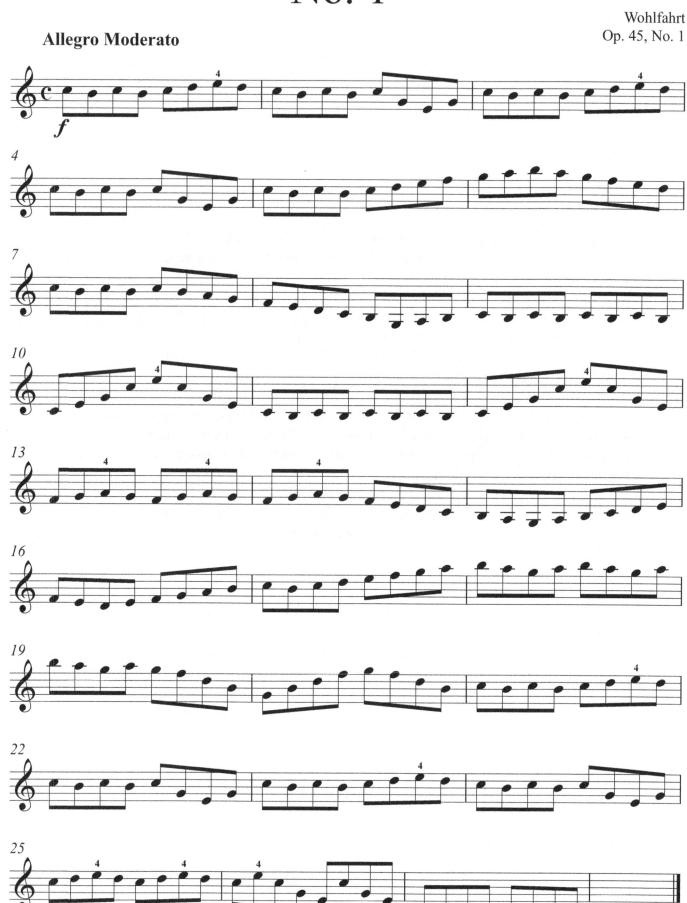

No. 2

Wohlfahrt
Op. 45, No. 2

Allegro Moderato

No. 3

Wohlfahrt
Op. 45, No. 3

Moderato

No. 4

Wohlfahrt
Op. 45, No. 4

Allegretto

No. 6

Wohlfahrt
Op. 45, No. 6

Moderato

No. 7

Wohlfahrt
Op. 45, No. 7

Allegro Moderato

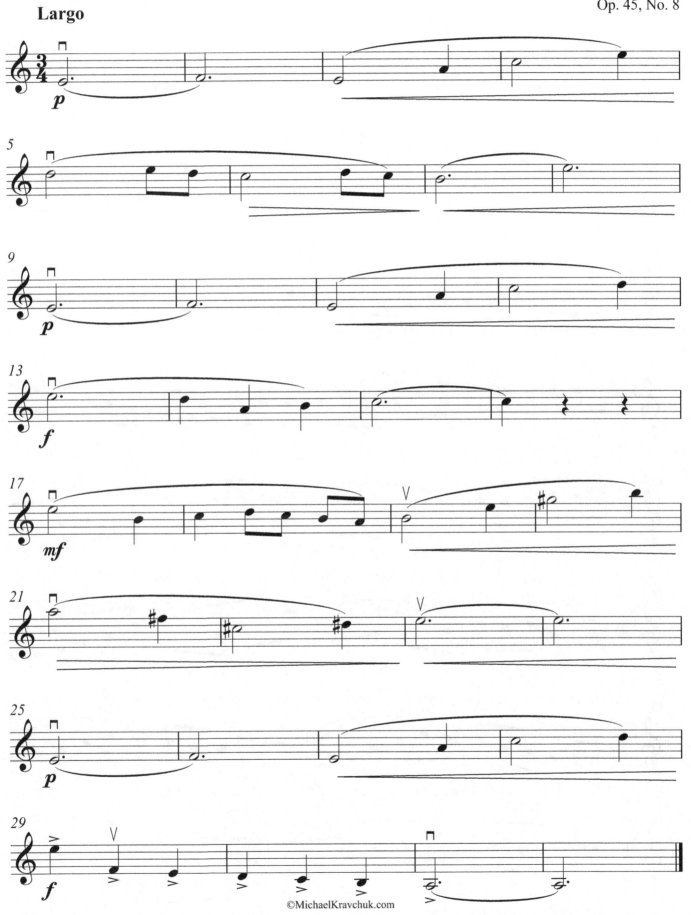

No. 9

Wohlfahrt
Op. 45, No. 9

Allegretto

No. 10

Wohlfahrt
Op. 45, No. 10

Moderato

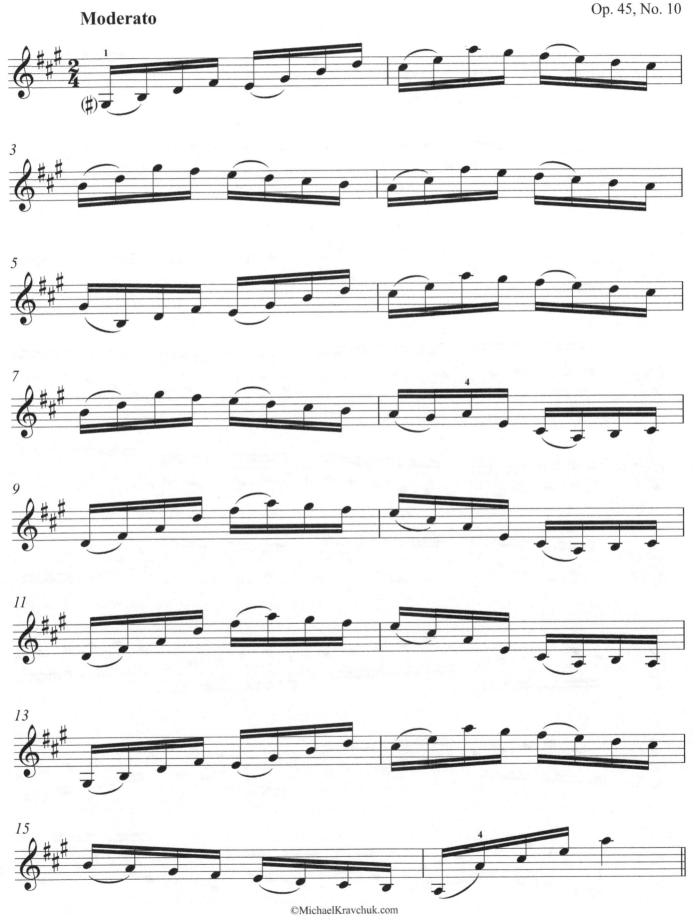

No. 11

Wohlfahrt
Op. 45, No. 11

Moderato

No. 12

Wohlfahrt
Op. 45, No. 12

Allegro

No. 13

Wohlfahrt
Op. 45, No. 13

No. 14

Allegro non tanto

Wohlfahrt
Op. 45, No. 14

No. 15

Wohlfahrt
Op. 45, No. 15

Allegro

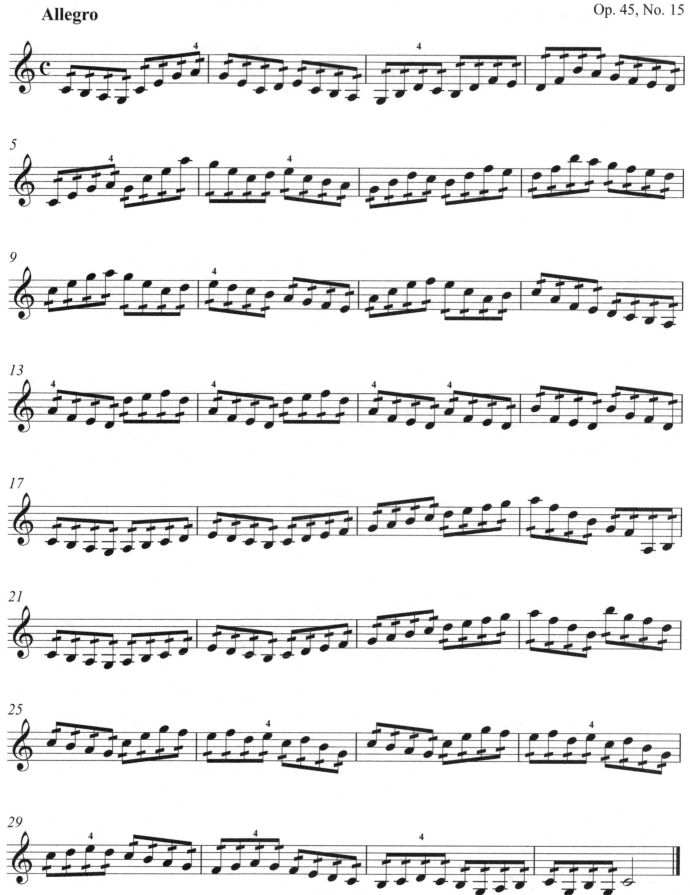

No. 16

Wohlfahrt
Op. 45, No. 16

Moderato

No. 18

Wohlfahrt
Op. 45, No. 18

Allegro

No. 19

Wohlfahrt
Op. 45, No. 19

Moderato

No. 21

Wohlfahrt
Op. 45, No. 21

Allegro

No. 22

Wohlfahrt
Op. 45, No. 22

Allegro

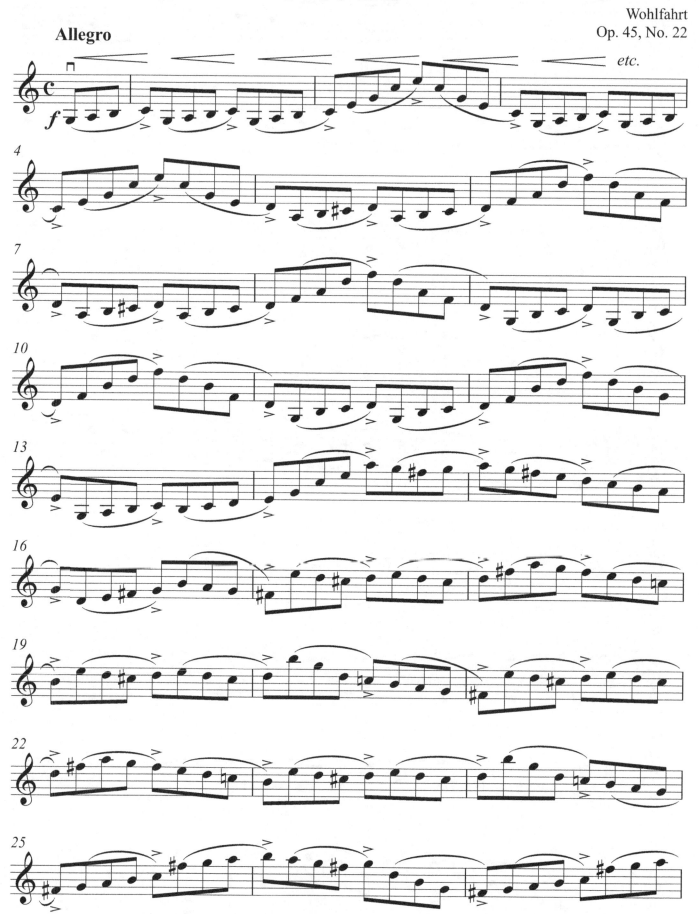

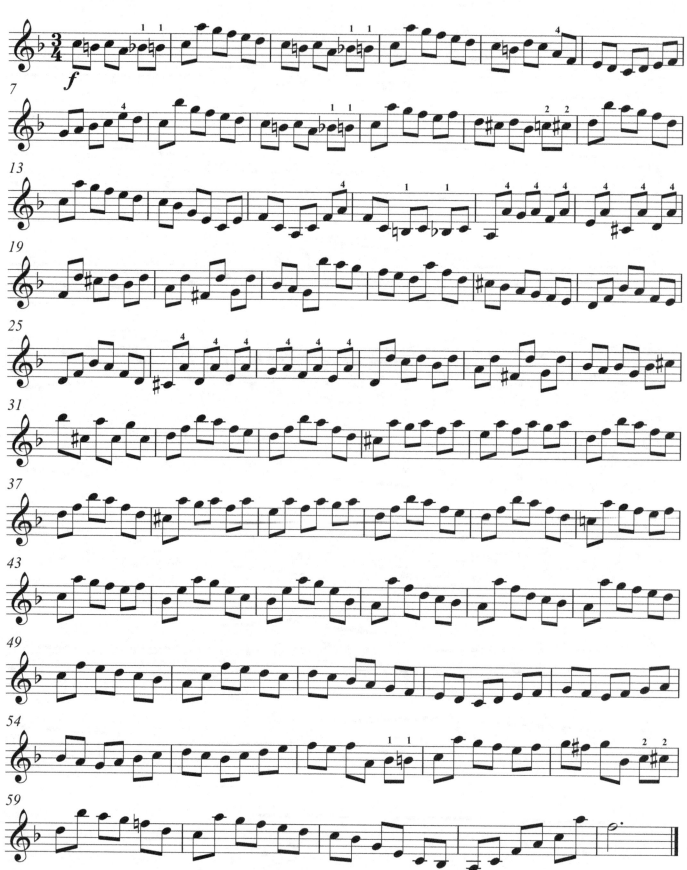

No. 24

Wohlfahrt
Op. 45, No. 24

Moderato assai

No. 25

Wohlfahrt
Op. 45, No. 25

No. 26

Wohlfahrt
Op. 45, No. 26

Allegro

No. 27

Wohlfahrt
Op. 45, No. 27

No. 28

Wohlfahrt
Op. 45, No. 28

Allegretto

No. 29

Wohlfahrt
Op. 45, No. 29

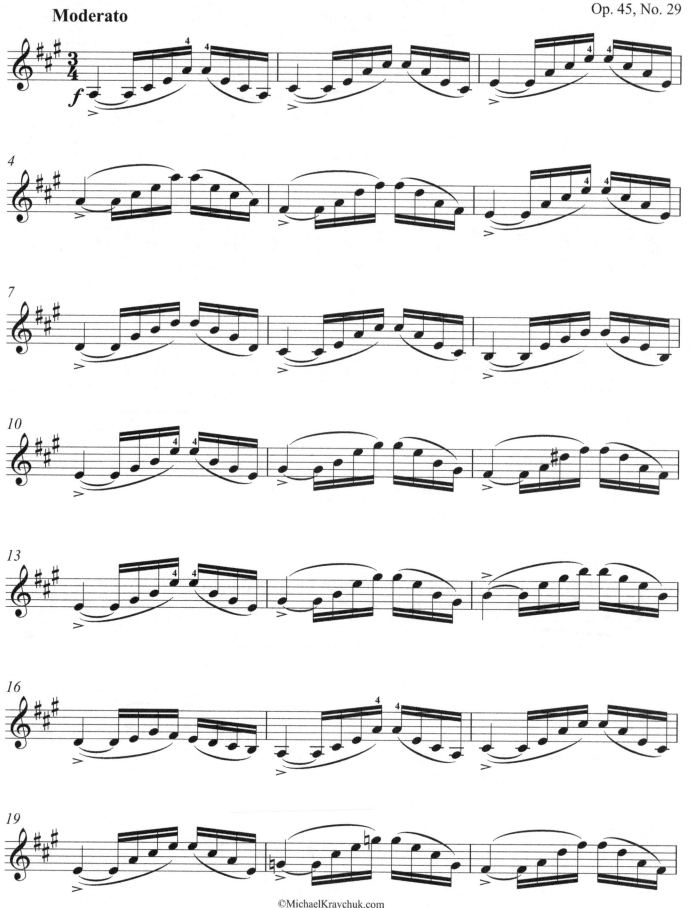

No. 30

Wohlfahrt
Op. 45, No. 30

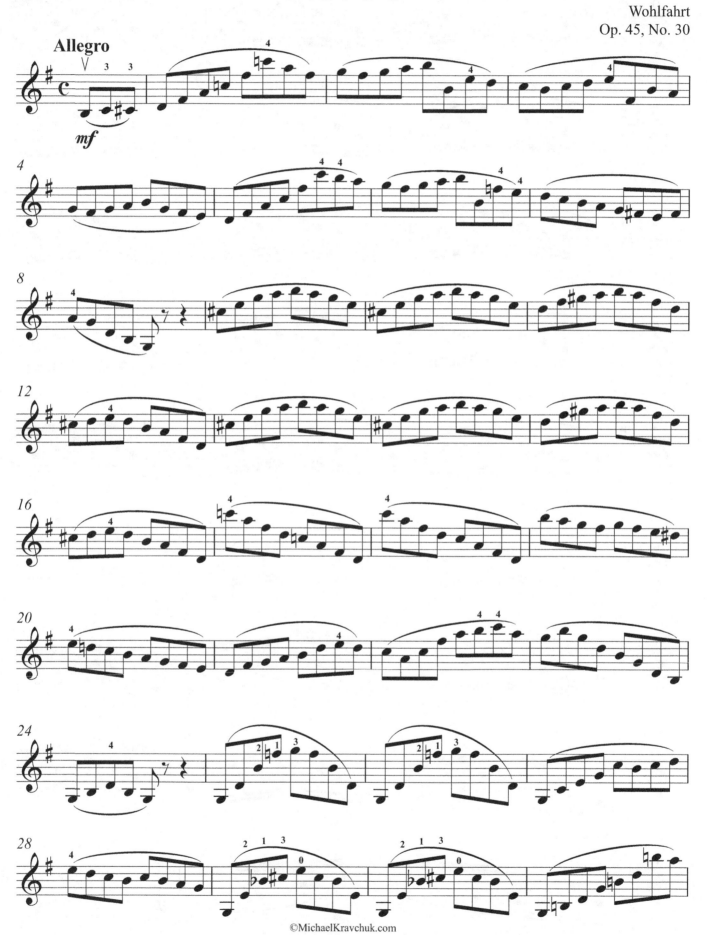

No. 31

Wohlfahrt
Op. 45, No. 31

Moderato

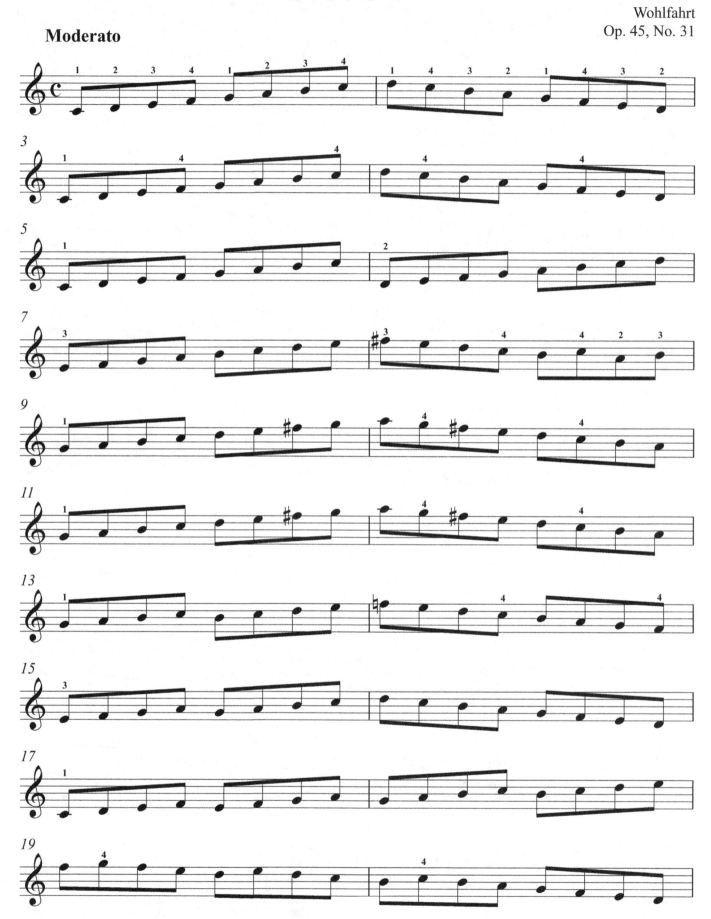

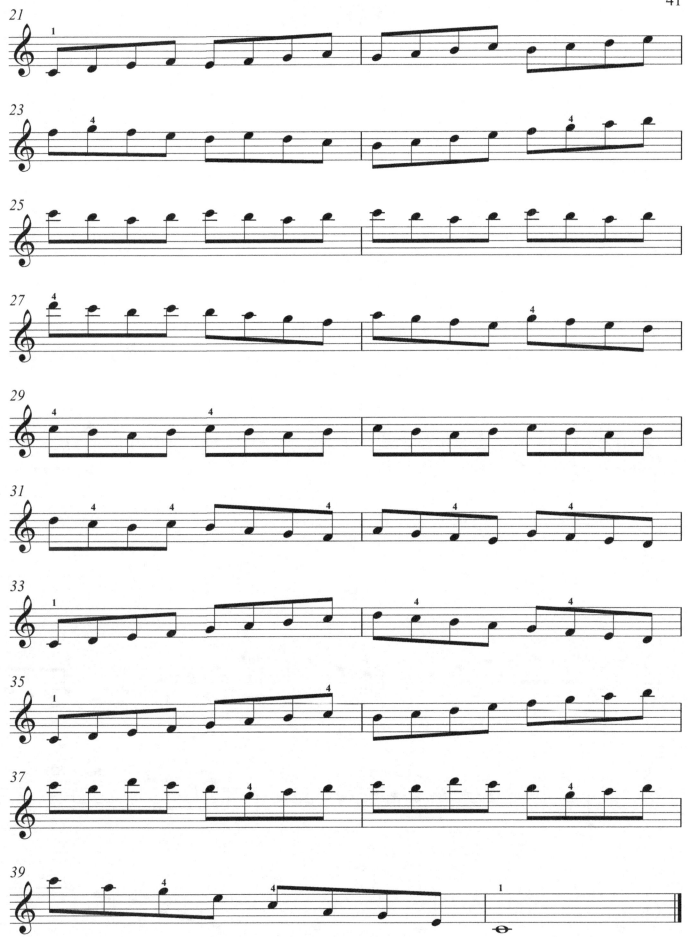

No. 33

Wohlfahrt
Op. 45, No. 33

Allegro Moderato

No. 34

Wohlfahrt
Op. 45, No. 34

Allegro

No. 35

Wohlfahrt
Op. 45, No. 35

Allegro

No. 37

Wohlfahrt
Op. 45, No. 37

No. 38

Wohlfahrt
Op. 45, No. 38

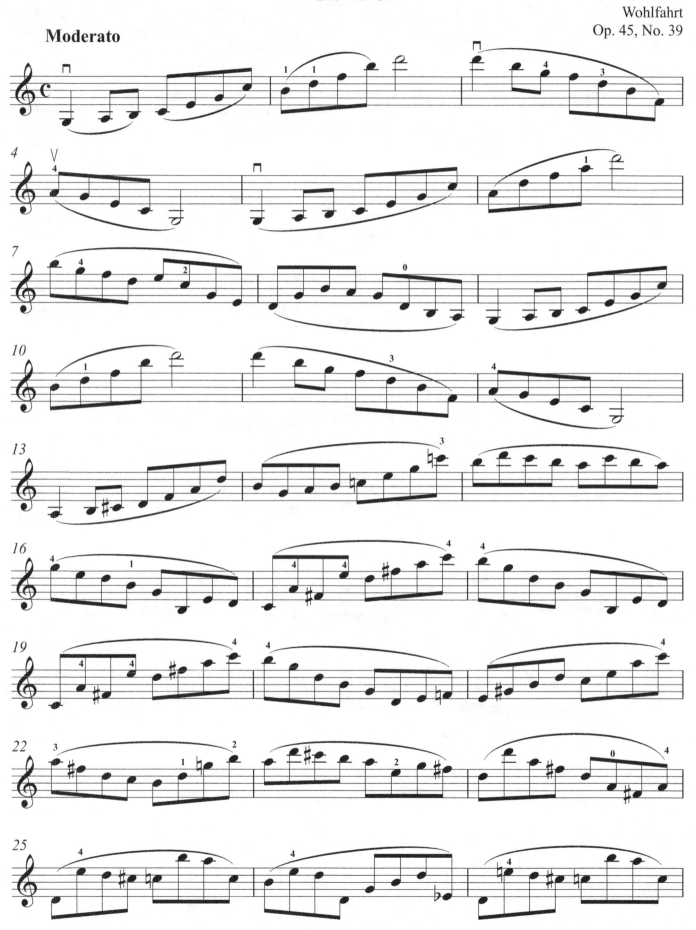

No. 40

Wohlfahrt
Op. 45, No. 40

Allegro scherzando

No. 41

Wohlfahrt
Op. 45, No. 41

Allegro moderato

No. 42

Wohlfahrt
Op. 45, No. 42

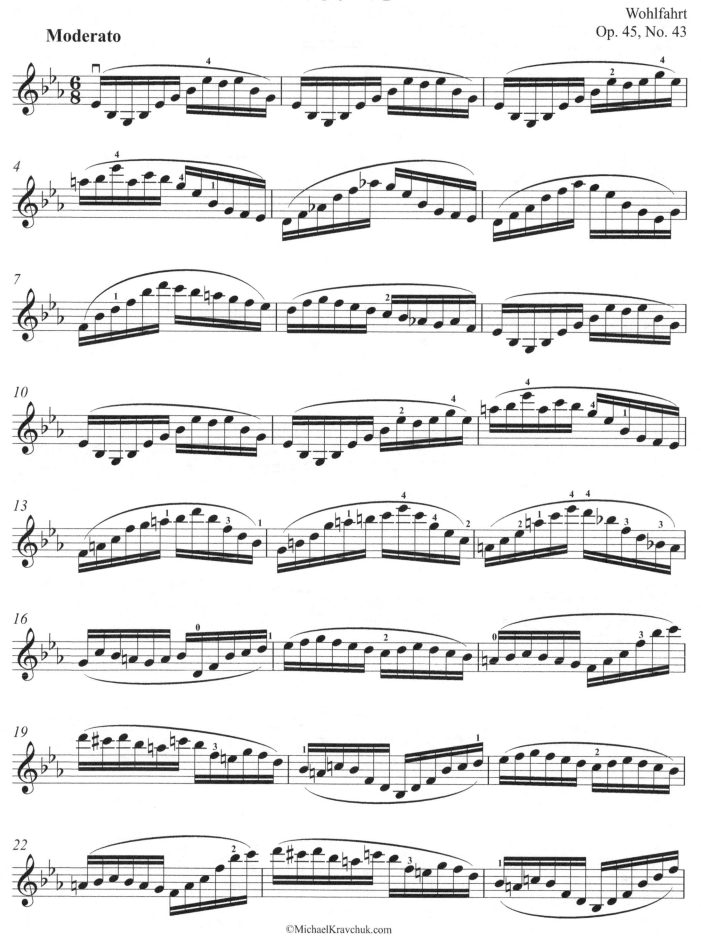

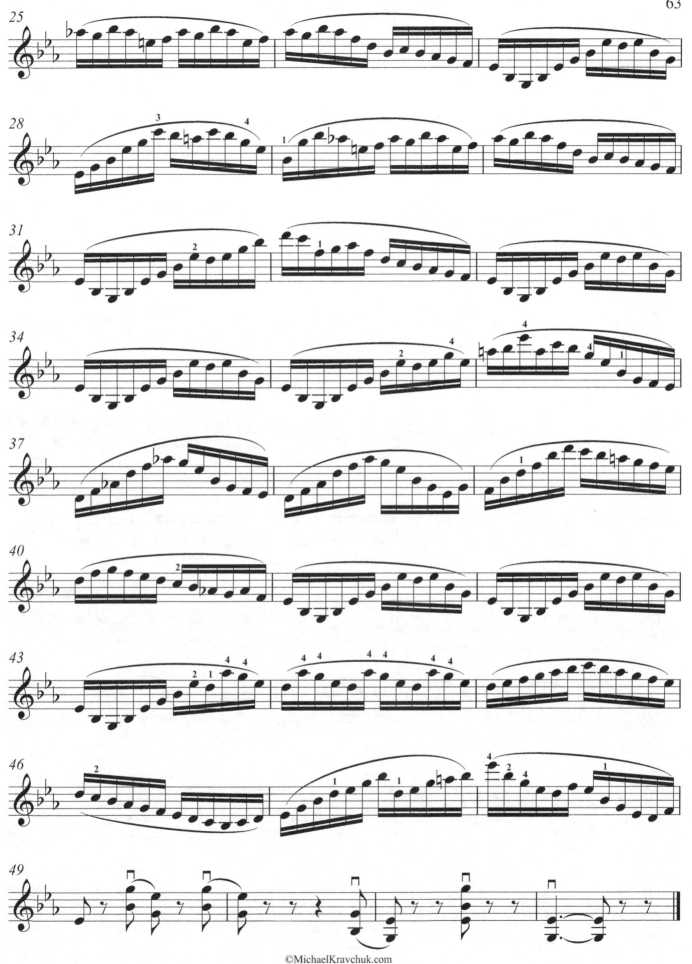

No. 44

Wohlfahrt
Op. 45, No. 44

Tempo di marcia

No. 45

Wohlfahrt
Op. 45, No. 45

Moderato

No. 46

Wohlfahrt
Op. 45, No. 46

Allegro

No. 47

Wohlfahrt
Op. 45, No. 47

Andante Cantabile

No. 48

Wohlfahrt
Op. 45, No. 48

Allegretto

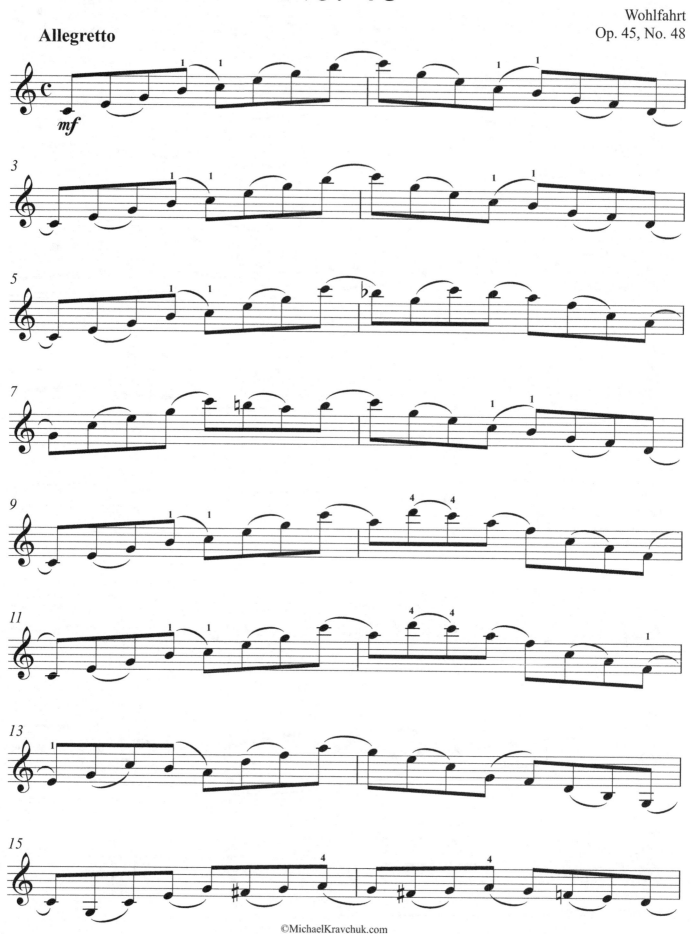

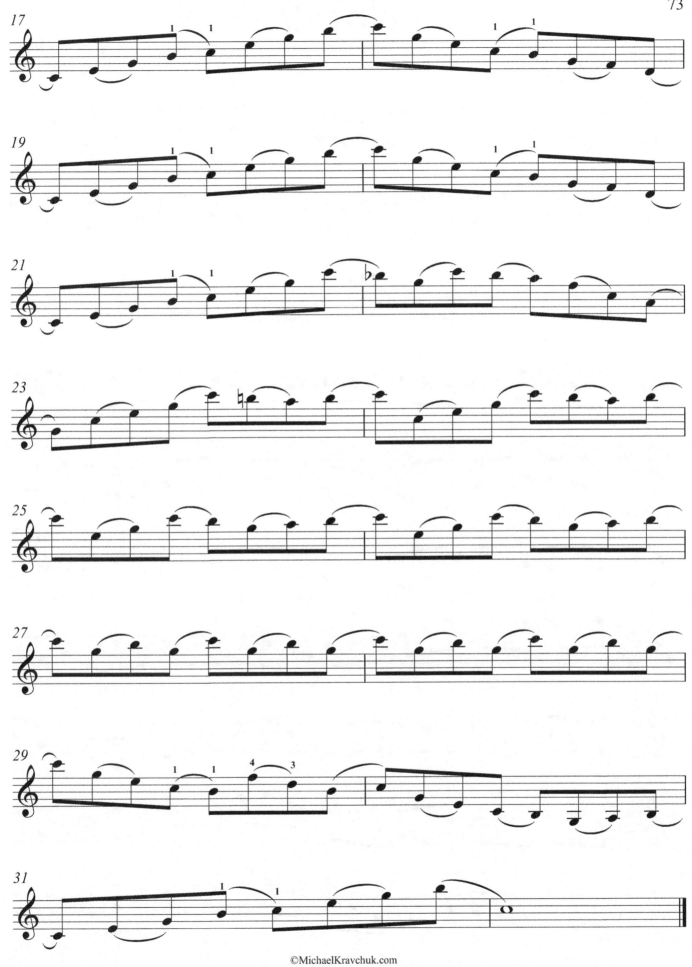

No. 49

Wohlfahrt
Op. 45, No. 49

Allegro

No. 50

Wohlfahrt
Op. 45, No. 50

Allegro

No. 51

Wohlfahrt
Op. 45, No. 51

Moderato

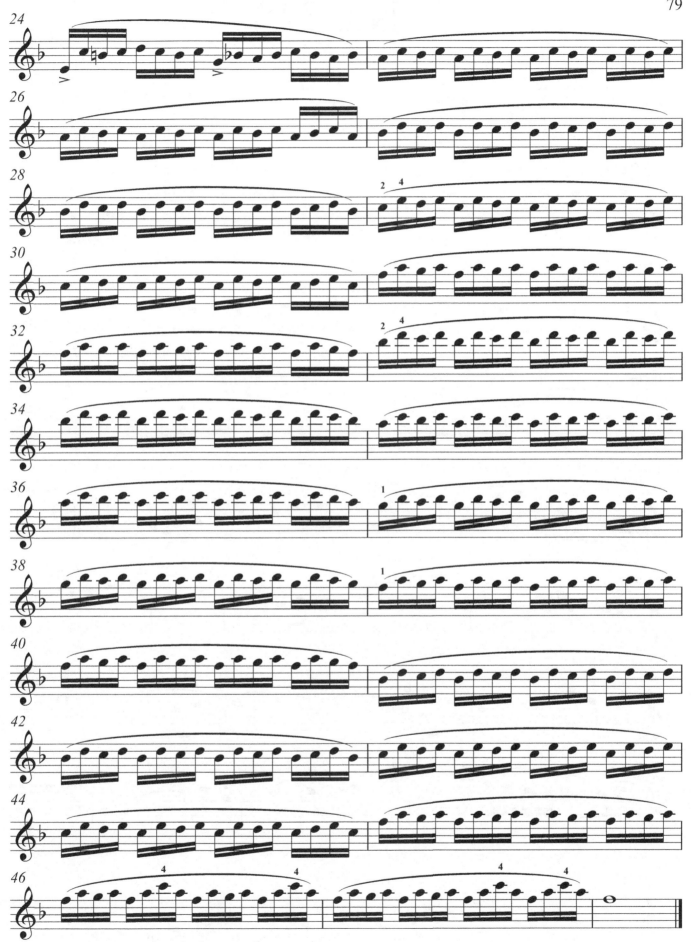

No. 53

Wohlfahrt
Op. 45, No. 53

Andante

No. 54

Wohlfahrt
Op. 45, No. 54

Allegro

No. 55

Wohlfahrt
Op. 45, No. 55

Allegro

No. 56

Wohlfahrt
Op. 45, No. 56

Andante

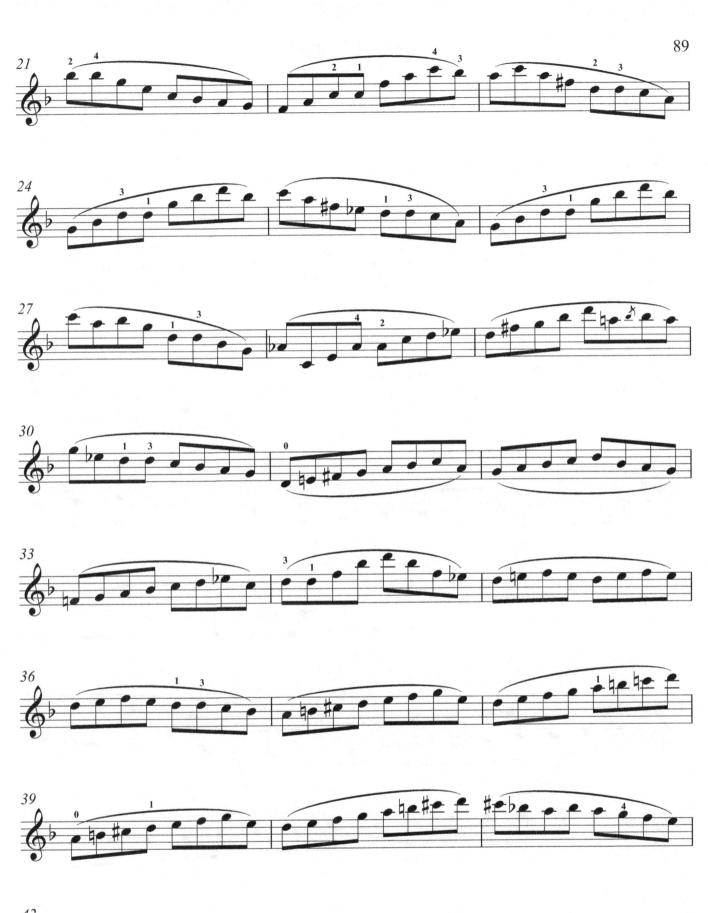

No. 58

Wohlfahrt
Op. 45, No. 58

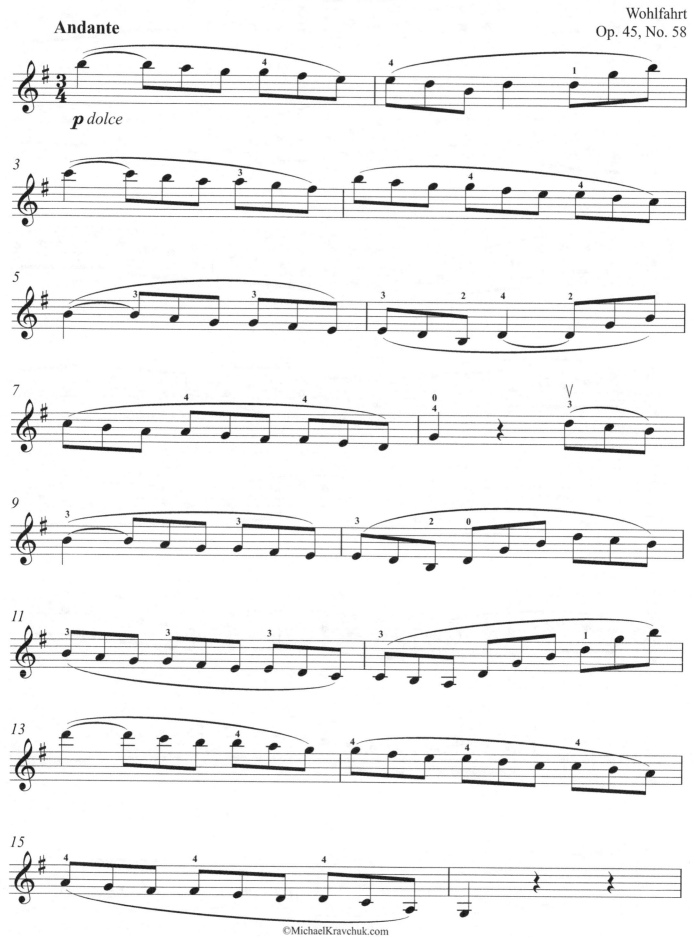

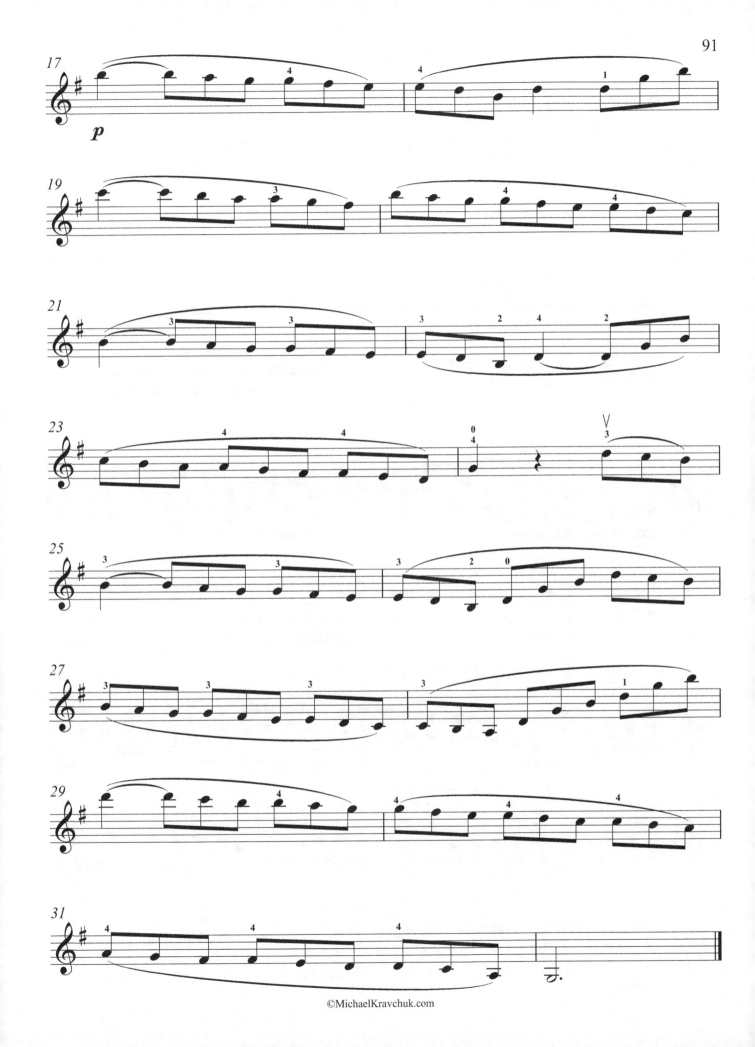

Made in the USA
Las Vegas, NV
16 March 2024

87320939R00052